To my son David. To help
his learning process

CW00672662

Robonauts® by NASA. RX78® by Sunrise Inc. PICO® by Sandia National Labs. Industrial Robot by Kuka® Robotics. HEXBUG® is a trademark of Innovation First Labs.Some pictures and information are property of their respective author, manufacturer company and/or copyright owner. They are cited on this book because of their relation and relevance. The information and brand names used here are solely for educational purposes and to preserve information about robot history for future generations.

 Robot Story

www.lt-automation.com
PH 305 914 5083
FAX 775 637 6825
Miami, FL, USA

Robot´s Parts

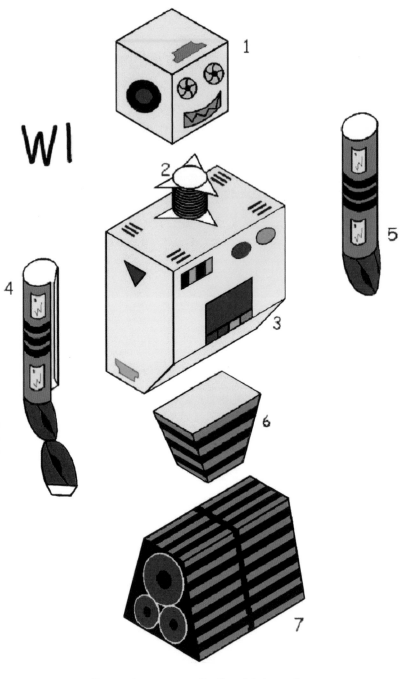

WI

Comming soon: Online University
www.onlinemediauniversity.com

Table of Contents

What is a Robot?

A Robot is a machine, with a computerized brain that can obey orders and sometimes do things by itself.

Robot is just a way to name those machines that can perform work very precisely and, sometimes, in repetitive ways.

Often They can also make their own autonomous decisions.

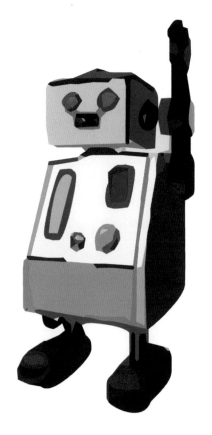

What a Robot is not

There are many machines that can look like Robots. But they are not. For example: A stove, a fridge, a microwave. All of these things ARE NOT Robots.

Machines and devices that can't do things by themselves, and that can't make simple decisions are not considered robots!

Are Robots dangerous?

Are you afraid of robots ?

In general, Robots are very nice with people. They are not made to harm people at all, but sometimes they can get a little crazy due to malfunctions.

A malfunction robot acts the same like when you are sick. When Robots are sick they don't do things right, but remember they never want to harm or scare you.

Where does the word ROBOT come from?

Karel Capec

Josef Capec

Several years ago (1919) in a country named Checoslovaquia, there was a writer named Karel Capec. He was thinking of writing theater plays.

He was doubting if it would be okay to use the word "Labori," to name the "Artificial Workers" on his play, so he asked his brother Josef, who was painting at that moment and without paying attention, his brother answered:

"Just call them Robots".

And that's how the word "Robot" was created.

How should a ROBOT act?

The Robots must follow three Main Directives known as Laws.

In order to prevent the humans from being harmed by Robots, a writer named ISAAC ASIMOV decided to clearly define the way a Robot should act.

He defined the

Three Laws of Robotics.

Isaac Asimov

If you like ROBOTs you must learn these laws very well.

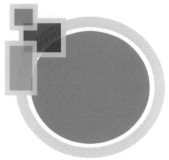

First law of robotics

"A Robot can't harm a human-being or allow a human being to be harmed through inaction."

A robot is here to protect you. It will not harm you in any way. If he realizes that someone or something is about to harm you, it will do whatever it takes to protect you, even if itself gets damaged.

What's this robot doing?

How could you explain the first law?

Second law of robotics

"A robot must obey orders from human beings, except when those order will conflict with the first law."

If you give an order to a robot it will do it immediately. Who do you obey orders from?

You must obey orders from your parents, the same way the robot respects and follows your orders. But, what happens when someone gives order to a robot to harm someone you love or care about?

The robot won't follow orders to harm people. This is because of the first law. Remember?

Third law of robotics

"A robot must protect its own existence as long as such protection doesn't conflict with the First or Second law."

Destroy!

I must protect the kid!

Nobody likes to get hurt! A Robot is no exception, they like to remain intact. If something or someone attacks a Robot, it will try to protect itself, but it will never act against a person.

My friend, be careful when giving orders to Robots! Be good and protect the existence of all living creatures and Robots.

What will the robot do to protect the kid?

Types of robots

There are several types of Robots that you will find in movies, TV shows, toys and industries.

You will learn how to recognize them once you understand the way they look and the kind of job they do.

It's possible that you have already seen them because you like movies, right?

The following pages will teach you how the robots are built. Try to remember their names. You will be happy to tell your friends about the types of robots.

Androids

An Android is a Robot that looks and acts like a human. Very few Robots can walk as humans. It's very difficult for Robots to walk.

Since Androids have legs and arms just like you, they can walk and grab things the same way you do.

Some of them can even play soccer!

Beams

These Robots are very basic, ugly and small. They respond to any situation in the environment like light or sound.

They are made from recycled parts using just a few components. They must receive the energy from the sun.

In order to capture the solar energy you have to use a device named Solar cell.

Cyborgs

This type of robots combine human and robotics parts. The word Cyborg comes from the three first letters of the words:

<u>Cyb</u>ernetics and <u>Org</u>anism.

Robots that have human parts are also called cyborgs.

Cybugs

The CYBUGs are small Robots that behave like living organisms. They look like the bugs you know, such as: flies, spiders and roaches.

The CYBUGs that move away from noise are called: NOISE PHOBIC CYBUGs. The ones that get close to noise are called: NOISE FOLLOWERS.

These robots have small mechanical and electronic parts. Makers give beautiful colors to cyber bugs, like the ones you see on the left side.

Industrial

These ones are Robots that work in factories.
They help in making things.

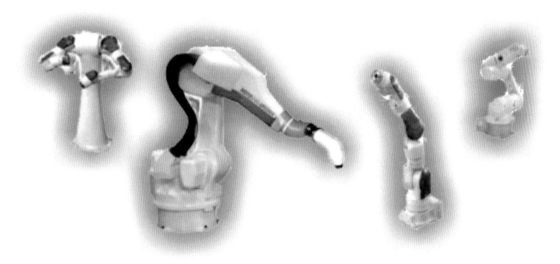

There are robots for assembling cars. some robots
are "mounting robots" which insert and put together
several pieces of electric devices, like video
games and computers.

Some jobs are very dangerous for people. In these
cases, persons are replaced with industrial robots.
For instance there robots that work in very
hot places.

Wheeled Robots

Robots with wheels or tires instead of legs, are known as wheeled Robots.

The wheels allow them to move very fast in all type of surfaces.

Some Robots use wheels to move similar to the ones found on war tanks.

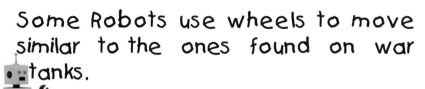

Biggest and strongest Industrial robot

This robot is 3,2 meters tall and can move things that weigh 1000 kilograms.

It's made by the German Company KUKA robotics.

World's smallest robot

The robot is named PICO and was made by Sandia National Labs. It's considered one of the world's smallest robots. It only measures 12.5 millimeters long.

It has its own batteries to run for 15 minutes before needing to recharge its power. It has a very small infrared sensor to detect any object placed in front.

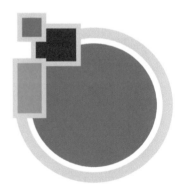

World's biggest robot statue

This robot is 18 meters tall and it is located in the Odamba Island in Tokyo to honor one of the Mobile Suit Gundam anime series characters.

Its name is RX78 and its code name is Gundam.

The robot statue is capable of moving its head.

World's first android robot design

Leonardo was born in Italy in 1452. He is considered a real Genius.

He was the first person who imagined and developed a robot with human form. It looked like a knight with armor.

Leonardo Da Vinci

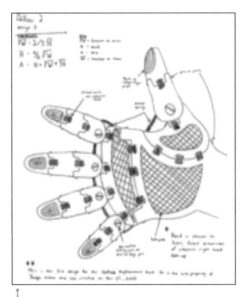

He also made a mechanical lion which that could walk. This one could also be considered a Robot.

His ideas and inventions were very innovative. They are now applied in modern science.

First Humanoid Robot in Space

The National Aeronautics and Space Administration (NASA) from United States, is developing ultra advanced robots to help Astronauts do their jobs in space.

These robots are called "Robonauts"

Future space missions will include a Robonaut as part of their crew.

New Technologies for Robotics

Muscle wires and Robotics. There are new products in the market which can change the way we conceive the world of Robots. One of them is a new metallic wire called NITINOL.

Imagine a wire similar to a hair strand. What is interesting about this wire is that it shortens in length, when it gets hot. The movement is similar to the one human muscles do. You can use a hair drier or connect it to an electric charge to apply heat.

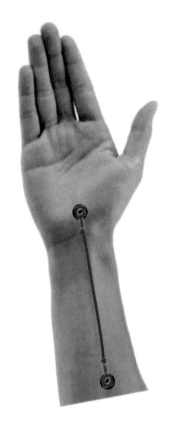

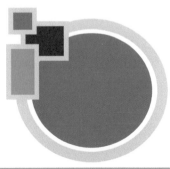

Vocabulary

Computerized:
That uses a computer

Repetitive:
That makes something several times.

Malfunction:
When a machine does not work the right way.

Play:
It's what actors present in a theater.

Artificial:
Not made by nature but by the man.

Law:
Something that becomes a rule that must be respected.

Inaction:
When nothing is done.

Conflict:
Two orders opposing to each other.

Protect:
To avoid that someone gets hurt.

Soccer:
A type of football played with a ball that can only be kicked by your feet or your head.

To Follow:
To go in the same direction of someone or something

Organism:
A form of life like a plant, a human, an animal, etc.

Phobic:
That rejects or doesn't like something.

Mechanical:
Something related to machines or tools.

Electronic:
Made of something that use electric current or require power source.

Environment:
Everything you see around you.

Energy:
What everybody needs to do a job.

Components:
The same as parts.

Recycled:
To use something that was already used or thrown.

Power:
Energy to move or work.

Assembling:
To put the parts all together.

Cybernetics:
The art of directing a course to look for and do something.

Kilograms:
A way or unit to describe how heavy is something.

Infrared:
Type of light you can't see.

Detect:
To know about the presence of something.

Code name:
A secret name.

Innovative:
Something that is new and that people like.

Astronauts:
Persons that work in space.

Crew:
Group of persons that control a vehicle or a ship.

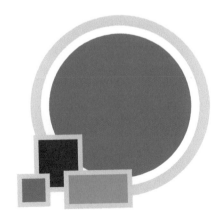

Printed in Great Britain
by Amazon